SUMMARY & ANALYSIS

OF

Lifespan

Why We Age—and Why We Don't Have To

A GUIDE TO
DAVID SINCLAIR'S BOOK

NOTE: This book is a summary and analysis and is meant as a companion to, not a replacement for, the original book.

SNAP Summaries is wholly responsible for this content and is not associated with the original author in any way. If you are the author, publisher, or representative of the original work, please contact info@snapsummaries.com with any questions or concerns.

Please follow this link to purchase a copy of the original book: https://amzn.to/2Mw3lRy

Copyright © 2019 by SNAP Summaries. All rights reserved. This book or parts thereof may not be reproduced in any form, stored in any retrieval system, or transmitted in any form by any means—electronic, mechanical, photocopy, recording, or otherwise—without prior written permission of the publisher, except as provided by United States of America copyright law. This book is intended as a companion to, not a replacement for the original book. SNAP Summaries is wholly responsible for this content and is not associated with the original author in any way.

TABLE OF CONTENTS

SYNOPSIS **1**

INTRODUCTION **2**

PART I: WHAT WE KNOW (THE PAST) **3**

CHAPTER 1: Viva Primordium 3

Key Takeaway: Human beings inherited the gene circuit that made early life forms super survivors. 3

Key Takeaway: The gene circuit that makes us great survivors is also the reason we age. 4

Key Takeaway: Aging is not caused by free-radical damage or mutations in DNA. 6

Key Takeaway: Aging is the loss of analog biological information. 6

CHAPTER 2: The Demented Pianist 7

Key Takeaway: Aging occurs when the epigenetic signalers that respond to cellular damage are overworked. 8

Key Takeaway: Aging can be slowed down and reversed by activating sirtuins. 9

CHAPTER 3: The Blind Epidemic 9

Key Takeaway: Treating one disease at a time does prolongs neither healthspan nor lifespan. 10

Key Takeaway: Aging is the biggest risk factor for all diseases. 11

PART II: WHAT WE'RE LEARNING (THE PRESENT) **12**

CHAPTER 4: Longevity Now 12

Key Takeaway: Limit calories to engage the survival circuit. 12

Key Takeaway: Replace animal protein with plant protein to improve your metabolic health markers. 13

Key Takeaway: Do vigorous exercise five times a week to stay younger at the cellular level. 14

Key Takeaway: Expose yourself to cold temperature to stimulate longevity genes. 15

CHAPTER 5: A Better Pill to Swallow 15

Key Takeaway: Compounds that inhibit mTOR, activate AMPK, and increase NAD levels boost health and longevity. 16

CHAPTER 6: Big Steps Ahead............................18

Key Takeaway: Drugs and vaccines that target zombie cells show potential to prolong vitality. 19

Key Takeaway: Yamanaka factors can reset the epigenome and reverse cellular age. 19

CHAPTER 7: The Age of Innovation 20

Key Takeaway: Genome sequencing is revolutionizing the future of medicine. 20

Key Takeaway: Biotrackers are key to optimizing health and boosting longevity. 22

PART III: WHERE WE'RE GOING (THE FUTURE).. 23

CHAPTER 8: The Shape of Things to Come 23

Key Takeaway: The transition to longer lives will worsen environmental degradation. 24

Key Takeaway: Longer lifespan will mean less social progress and less social security. 24

Key Takeaway: Mankind will renovate in response to a growing population and make the world an even better place. 25

CHAPTER 9: A Path Forward 27

Key Takeaway: Defining aging as a disease will speed up the innovations that will prolong healthy lifespan. 27

EDITORIAL REVIEW 29

BACKGROUND ON DAVID ANDREW SINCLAIR 32

SYNOPSIS

In his book *Lifespan: Why We Age—and Why We Don't Have To*, David A. Sinclair reveals how aging occurs in human beings and other life forms and how it can be slowed, halted, and even reversed.

Humankind, Sinclair laments, has accepted aging as an inevitable part of life only because it doesn't know better. Not very long ago, we thought diseases like diabetes and cancer were inevitable and irreversible; we think the same of aging—the mother of all diseases—because that is all we have known. Until now.

In what he calls the Information Theory of Aging, Sinclair postulates that we age because environmental stressors break our DNA, and this cellular assault destabilizes our genome, disrupts our epigenome, and causes our cells to lose their identity and malfunction. Through such interventions as intermittent fasting and high-intensity training, we can activate the longevity genes that counter cellular degradation. In this way, we can extend our healthy years and slow down aging. Sinclair points out that drugs and therapies that mimic the effects of these interventions are already being developed. Treating aging, he predicts, is going to be easier than curing cancer.

Sinclair imagines a not-too-distant future where half of us live to be 150 and beyond, but without the frailty or disease we now associate with old age.

INTRODUCTION

We are living longer than ever before. But the quality of our lives has barely improved. Certainly not the quality of our last decades. Instead of using the advances we have made in technology and medicine to extend our youth, we are using them to postpone death. Anyone unlucky enough to live to be a hundred has to put up with physical impairment, innumerable diseases, and a seemingly endless cocktail of drugs.

But this is about to change. Recent discoveries in human biology point to the fact that we don't have to be weighed down by the pressure of a ticking clock. We can add decades of youth to our lives; we can increase not just our lifespan, but our healthspan—the amount of life without disease, frailty, or disability. We can be healthy, active, and happy past our 90s because there is no biological law that puts a limit to how long we can be healthy or how long we can live. By the turn of the next century, anyone who lives to be 120 years old will be said to have had an average lifespan.

PART I: WHAT WE KNOW (THE PAST)

CHAPTER 1: VIVA PRIMORDIUM

Four billion years ago, the earth was nothing more than a hot and volcanic mass. Its surface was covered with oceans of salty water, and its atmosphere was filled with a mix of nitrogen, carbon dioxide, and methane. As water pooled to thermal vents, organic molecules that came to earth on the backs of meteorites dissolved and grew into the first RNA molecules. The first cell membranes—and, consequently, the early life forms—developed as fatty acids swathed these molecules.

These early microscopic life forms evolved quickly, but they had to compete for survival amidst intense volcanic activity and prolonged dry seasons. The species that would dominate this harsh environment and go on to become the ancestor of all future life forms on earth would have to develop a special genetic survival mechanism.

Key Takeaway: Human beings inherited the gene circuit that made early life forms super survivors.

The author calls the theoretical species that won the supremacy fight *Magna Superstes*, Latin for 'great survivor.' The gene circuit it developed to survive was simple: gene A would stop cells from reproducing when conditions were unfavorable, and gene B would produce a protein that turned off gene A when it was safe again to reproduce. Gene B would also help repair DNA.

The cell's DNA can be broken by radiation and any other extreme environmental condition. When the DNA in the cells of *M. Superstes* was broken, the protein that gene B produced would vacate its role of silencing gene A and go to help with DNA repair. When the silencing protein left, gene A would be turned on, and the cell would stop reproduction. When DNA repair was completed, the silencing protein would head back home and sit on gene A. With gene A silenced again, reproduction could resume.

This gene circuit was crucial to the survival of *M. Superstes* because in the brutal conditions of primitive earth, any organism that attempted to repair DNA and reproduce at the same time would overburden itself and die. Every living thing today, including human beings, inherited an advanced form of this gene circuit. This circuit directs energy where it is needed most and only permits reproduction when conditions are favorable.

Key Takeaway: The gene circuit that makes us great survivors is also the reason we age.

The survival circuit we inherited from *M. Superstes* has evolved by leaps and bounds. The human genome has not two but more than two dozen genes that make up the survival circuit. These genes communicate with one another and tell cells to go into preservation mode when times are bad and reproduce when times are good. They can be manipulated not just to make us healthier, but to extend our lifespan, as well.

Several pathways have evolved to activate the survival mechanisms and protect the body when times are tough. There is a kinase or enzyme called target of rapamycin (TOR), another enzyme called AMP-activated protein kinase (AMPK), and a family of proteins called sirtuins. Some biological stressors, such as rigorous exercise, intermittent fasting, and cold exposure, activate these pathways without damaging DNA. When these pathways are activated, they force the body to go into preservation mode and activate the genes that code for health, disease resistance, and longevity.

Every cell in the body produces sirtuins. In mammals, there are seven sirtuins: SIRT1 to SIRT7. These enzymes, which are descendants of gene B, change the packaging of DNA and turn genes on and off as needed. This way, they control not just reproduction and DNA repair, but health and survival, as well. In lab experiments, activating the sirtuins in mice improves DNA repair, increases their exercise endurance, and extends their lifespan. If the activity of sirtuins is compromised, mammals become vulnerable to disease and degeneration.

To function, sirtuins require a molecule called nicotinamide adenine dinucleotide (NAD). As we age, we lose NAD, and this loss undermines the activity of sirtuins. This may be the reason we become frail and prone to disease as we get older.

Key Takeaway: Aging is not caused by free-radical damage or mutations in DNA.

In the 1960s, Denham Harman proposed that aging was caused by unpaired electrons—or free radicals—that damaged DNA and precipitated the loss of crucial genetic information. If his theory was correct, antioxidants would counter the action of free radicals and extend the lifespan of animal subjects. However, in hundreds of experiments conducted in the 1970s and 80s, antioxidants only increased the average lifespan of test subjects, not their maximum lifespan. Test animals were living a few weeks longer than usual, but none was breaking the species' known age limit. In other lab experiments, increasing free-radical damage in mice did not accelerate their aging. Yet, despite these experiments, the free-radical theory of aging is still a popular theory.

If mutations cause aging by steering the loss of crucial genetic information, one would expect that the clones of older animals would also be older animals. However, when older animals are cloned, they produce offspring that do not show any signs of premature aging. These clones go on to live normal, healthy lifespans, and this proves that older animals have not lost any genetic information.

Key Takeaway: Aging is the loss of analog biological information.

There are two types of biological information: digital information, which is stored as DNA, and analog information, which is basically the epigenome. Both systems of information evolved for different but complimentary purposes: the digital system to store long-term genetic information, and the analog system to store data that could be adapted to changing environmental conditions.

The epigenome is made up of chemical compounds that tell the genome what to do. It acts like a software; it tells genes where they should be active or inactive at certain times, and this on-off switch determines the form that newly divided cells take. Without this software, skin cells, blood cells, and some other types of cells would lose their identity and become other types of cells. Consequently, tissues and organs would lose their functions and fail.

Cells retain their digital information as people age because DNA is the equivalent of a digital file that can be copied over and over again with great accuracy. Analog information, however, is degraded over time by gravity, cosmic rays, magnetic fields, and other environmental forces. As it is battered by these forces, the analog system becomes the equivalent of a scratched DVD. Frailty, pain, and disease—the hallmarks of aging—set in as analog information is lost.

CHAPTER 2: THE DEMENTED PIANIST

All cells have the same DNA. What differentiates their function is the epigenome. It is the control system that tells cells what genes to turn on and what genes to keep turned off. If you think of the genome as a grand piano, each key would represent one of our 20,000 genes. Every key—

which could be played in several different ways—would make a different sound. The epigenome would be the pianist.

If, for some reason, the pianist kept missing notes or playing extra keys, she would ruin the concerto. In the same way, the music of our lives—our health and youth—is ruined by the chaos that ensues when the epigenome is disrupted.

Key Takeaway: Aging occurs when the epigenetic signalers that respond to cellular damage are overworked.

Radiation, X-rays, chemicals, and other environmental factors break DNA and disrupt the epigenome. When sirtuins move in to repair DNA, they pause their original epigenetic function—which is to control genes and ensure cells keep their identity and function optimally—and only get back to this function when the damage they go to repair is fixed.

While sirtuins are away, genes that are supposed to be switched off turn on, and those supposed to be on go off. If there are constant assaults on DNA, sirtuins don't make their way back to their original posts. Sometimes they return to the wrong place and silence the wrong genes. The cells whose health they should be regulating—and the ones they shouldn't be regulating but are now regulating—lose their identity and malfunction. The chaos that follows shows up as aging.

When the genetic signalers that control the epigenome are disrupted in lab subjects, the effect on aging is clear. Lab mice engineered to lack SIRT6, for example, age and die faster than their peers because their cells lose the ability to repair DNA breaks. Adding extra copies of the sirtuin genes SIRT1 and SIRT6 boosts their health and extends their lifespan.

Key Takeaway: Aging can be slowed down and reversed by activating sirtuins.

In lab experiments, feeding mice with molecules that boosted their levels of NAD increased the activity of their sirtuins and renewed their vitality. Lab mice that were 20 months old (the equivalent of 65 human years) were suddenly doing three-kilometer marathons on a treadmill—an unbelievable achievement for mice that old.

When the NAD-boosting molecules activated the SIRT1 enzyme, endothelial cells pushed their way to muscle areas that were getting insufficient blood flow, new tiny blood vessels formed, and increased oxygen flow neutralized the lactic acid in muscles and reversed the frailty of the mice. Activating sirtuins stabilized the epigenome and countered the hallmarks of aging.

CHAPTER 3: THE BLIND EPIDEMIC

As we grow older, we develop wrinkles, our hair turns grey, joints ache, and ailments that were once rare and easy to recover from become common and increasingly life-threatening. Among teenagers, for example, hip fractures are rare and almost always heal. Half of the senior citizens who suffer hip fractures die within six months. The older we get, it seems, the more likely it is for an injury or illness to push us to the grave. In this way, aging increases the probability of death more than any other disease. Yet there are no public health campaigns to fight it, and not nearly as much research dedicated to it as to cancer or heart disease.

We have accepted aging and its symptoms—including Alzheimer's, heart disease, and osteoporosis—as an inevitable part of life only because we don't know better. We are only now realizing that aging is a disease that can be treated.

Key Takeaway: Treating one disease at a time prolongs neither healthspan nor lifespan.

Most hospitals today have medical specialties, each occupying its own floor, and independent research wings. This structure reflects modern medicine's fixation with treating medical conditions one at a time. While this model worked well in the early days of modern medicine, it does not work well today.

Treating one disease does not make it likely that a person will be healthier or less likely that a person will die from another disease. If anything, treating one disease can exacerbate the risk of another. Chemotherapy, for example, can increase the risk of developing other cancers.

Treating one disease does not increase lifespan, either; it merely reduces the chances of dying of *that* disease. If all cardiovascular diseases and all forms of cancer were eradicated, we would add just 4 years to the average American lifespan because aging would still increase—rather exponentially—the risk of other causes of death. If we were genuinely interested in increasing both health and lifespan, we would invest more in medicine that combats aging and less in research or treatment of individual diseases.

Key Takeaway: Aging is the biggest risk factor for all diseases.

Smoking increases the risk of getting cancer by five times. Being 50 years old increases the same risk by a hundred times, and being 70 increases this risk a thousand-fold. There are public health campaigns, legislations, punitive taxes to prevent the fivefold increase in risk and almost no investments to combat the hundred- and thousand-fold risk.

Government policies and healthcare systems should be more focused on combating aging than any other disease. It makes more sense to invest more in the problem that impacts everyone than the problem that impacts small populations.

PART II: WHAT WE'RE LEARNING (THE PRESENT)

CHAPTER 4: LONGEVITY NOW

Exerting the good kind of cellular stress on our bodies is good for the epigenome because it activates the longevity pathway. It stimulates AMPK, boosts NAD levels, and activates the sirtuins. When they are stimulated, these longevity pathways keep other types of cellular damage in check and, consequently, boost both health and lifespan.

The bad kind of stress that exacerbates cellular wear and tear—and which you should avoid—is induced by smoking and exposure to pollution, PCBs and other chemicals in plastics, and radiation from UV, gamma, and X-rays.

Key Takeaway: Limit calories to engage the survival circuit.

Calorie restriction is good for health and longevity. Studies conducted since the 1930s have shown that restricting calories—but not too much as to cause malnutrition—boosts the longevity of all life forms, including rodents, yeast, and fruit flies. In experiments where people have been put on diets with significantly less calories than the typical diet, results have indicated a drop of between 20 and 30 percent in blood pressure, blood sugar levels, and cholesterol levels.

Calories restriction works because it engages the survival circuit. It stimulates longevity genes, and these genes boost cellular defenses and minimize changes in the epigenome. Limiting food intake to 12 to 25 percent fewer calories than is usually recommended for a healthy lifestyle significantly improves health—as evidenced by changes in blood biomarkers—and slows down aging.

You don't need to take on a strict life of calorie restriction to get these benefits; intermittent fasting has been shown to work even better. In one study that ran for three months, participants who took normal food portions and went on a calorie-restricted diet five days a month—they ate mostly vegetable soup, energy bars, and supplements—lost weight, lowered their blood pressure, and had lower levels of a hormone called insulin-like growth factor 1 (IGF-1). Levels of this hormone are linked to longevity and can be used to estimate how long a person will live.

Almost any intermittent fasting regimen—skipping breakfast and taking late lunch, eating 75 percent fewer calories two days a week, skipping food a few days a week, or skipping food an entire week each quarter—engages longevity genes, boosts health, and extends healthspan.

Key Takeaway: Replace animal protein with plant protein to improve your metabolic health markers.

Meat contains all of the nine essential amino acids. However, studies have shown that diets rich in animal products—especially processed red meats—pose a high risk of cardiovascular disease and a variety of cancers.

Plants provide limited amounts of amino acids. This is a good thing, because a limited amount of amino acids induces the good stress that engages survival circuits. It inhibits mTOR, which reprograms cells to spend less resources dividing and more resources repairing. If you limit your consumption of branched-chain amino acids—which are found in beef, poultry, dairy, and eggs—you can significantly improve your blood glucose levels and other metabolic health markers.

Key Takeaway: Do vigorous exercise five times a week to stay younger at the cellular level.

A low-protein, vegetable-rich diet may increase your lifespan but to maximize the effect of this regimen, you need to subject your body to physical stress. Studies show that running five miles a week can reduce the risk of death by 40 percent and overall mortality by 45 percent.

High-intensity interval training—the kind that induces deep, rapid breathing and causes you to break a sweat—improves blood flow and lung and heart function and changes the body at the cellular level. It raises NAD levels and activates the sirtuin genes that extend telomeres and guard against cellular degradation. Studies show that the telomeres of people who jog at least 30 minutes five days a week are longer and look about a decade younger than those of people who don't exercise.

Key Takeaway: Expose yourself to cold temperature to stimulate longevity genes.

Cold temperature stimulates longevity genes, activates the mitochondria in brown fat, and enhances the function of this fat. Studies show that animals with abundant brown fat have more of the sirtuin SIRT3 and lower rates of diabetes, obesity, and Alzheimer's disease. Studies also show that the function of brown fat is enhanced in genetically engineered Ames dwarf mice, and this may help explain why they live longer than other mice.

You can boost the production and function of brown fat by walking outside in a T-shirt on a cold winter day, exercising in the cold, or leaving a window open overnight.

CHAPTER 5: A BETTER PILL TO SWALLOW

The three main longevity pathways—mTOR, AMPK, and sirtuins—activate the survival circuit to protect the body in harsh conditions. Low-calorie and plant-based diets, intense exercise, and cold exposure activate these pathways and, consequently, boost the health, disease resistance, and longevity of organisms. But these measures are not the only way to engage the longevity pathways. Molecules that mimic the effect of these stress inducers can also be used to boost health and longevity.

Key Takeaway: Compounds that inhibit mTOR, activate AMPK, and increase NAD levels boost health and longevity.

Among the compounds known to extend life, the one that shows the most potential is rapamycin. This compound, which is used to suppress the immune system and prevent organ transplant rejection, interacts with mTOR to inhibit its function. It is safe in small or intermittent doses but toxic to kidneys when taken in high doses over prolonged periods. In lab studies, rapamycin has had a significant effect on the longevity of yeast cells and mice. Yeast cells have a short budding lifespan; only a few yeast cells are viable after six weeks. Fed with rapamycin, however, half of yeast cells are still heathy at week six. Mice in the last months of their normal lives live between 9 and 14 percent longer when given small doses of rapamycin. This extra lifespan is the equivalent of a decade in human years.

Another pharmaceutical intervention that shows potential to prolong lifespan is metformin, a drug used to treat type 2 diabetes. This cheap, generic drug extends the lifespan of lab mice by 6 percent, which is the equivalent of five additional human years. Mice put on this drug also have lower LDL cholesterol levels, improved physical performance, and a lower risk of getting cancer. Metformin limits metabolic reactions in mitochondria and slows down the rate at which cells convert food to energy. AMPK, which responds to low energy levels and restores mitochondria, is activated by this mechanism. Metformin also induces the production of NAD and, consequently, activates sirtuins and other aging defenses. In a study of metformin users, researchers found that the drug reduced the likelihood of frailty by 24 percent and the risk of dementia, cardiovascular disease, and cancer by significant margins.

There are several sirtuin-activating compounds that have been shown to boost health and prolong lifespan. A polyphenol called fisetin and a molecule called butein stimulate SIRT1 and make it work ten times as fast. Resveratrol, an antioxidant found in red wine, has structure similar to that of these compounds but performs even better. In experiments, yeast cells fed resveratrol grew slowly and lived the equivalent of 50 extra human years. Resveratrol also protected lab mice from cancers, inflammatory diseases, and heart disease and prolonged their lifespan by 20 percent. This compound extended the lifespan of organisms by mimicking the effect of calorie restriction.

NAD boosters are superior to these sirtuin-activating compounds because they activate all seven sirtuins in mammals. In humans, a form of vitamin B3 called nicotinamide riboside (NR) is converted into a compound called nicotinamide mononucleotide (NMN)—the same compound found in broccoli, avocado, and other foods—which is converted into NAD. Feeding a lab animal food with NR or NMN boosts its levels of NAD as much as if it were fasting or engaging in rigorous exercise. Research shows that NMN can restore NAD levels in old mice and increase their endurance. NMN also increases the speed, coordination, strength, and memory of old mice and helps protect against neurodegeneration and kidney damage. Mice fed NMN live longer than peers who are not on a similar regimen.

NAD boosters work by inducing just enough stress to activate longevity genes and reduce the epigenetic noise that causes aging. This effect is demonstrated by their ability to reverse infertility, one of the main hallmarks of aging. Studies have shown that NAD boosters can restore the fertility of old horses and old mice. Menopausal women taking supplemental NMN have also been reported to get their periods again.

CHAPTER 6: BIG STEPS AHEAD

One of the main marks of aging is the accumulation of senescent or "zombie" cells. These are cells that have ceased reproduction but refuse to die. The telomeres of human cells are eroded by each replication. After about forty to sixty divisions, cells lose important genetic information and can no longer divide. The zombie cells that hang around release proteins called cytokines that cause inflammation in surrounding cells. Cytokines also cause other cells to dysfunction and become zombies. The more the healthy cells in the surrounding area try to repair the damage caused by zombie cells, the more they destabilize the epigenome.

It is difficult to undo the damage in zombie cells. The best approach to restore the health of organisms inundated with zombie cells is to kill off these cells. By so doing, it is possible to stave off the frailty, memory loss, macular degeneration, and cancers associated with old age.

Key Takeaway: Drugs and vaccines that target zombie cells show potential to prolong vitality.

Small-molecule drugs called senolytics induce a cellular death program that kills senescent cells. In lab experiments, these drugs have extended the lifespan of mice by 36 percent. Human trials in which senolytics are used to treat glaucoma and osteoarthritis—conditions whose underlying cause is the accumulation of senescent cells—are still in progress.

In the future, it may also be possible to vaccinate against aging. Senescent cells, like cancer cells, are usually invisible to the immune system because they hide behind proteins that fool the immune system into thinking they are healthy cells. In a few years, there will be vaccines that take those proteins away and expose senescent cells.

Key Takeaway: Yamanaka factors can reset the epigenome and reverse cellular age.

Alternatively, cells can be reprogramed so that they don't lose their identity and become zombies. In 2006, Japanese stem cell researcher Shinya Yamanaka discovered a set of four genes that could turn adult cells into pluripotent stem cells. In effect, he discovered a way to make adult cells look and behave like embryonic stem cells that could develop into any other cell type. Using the reprogramming factors Yamanaka discovered—which are commonly referred to as Yamanaka factors—researchers can take adult skin cells, reprogram them, and use the new cells to grow blood cells, liver cells, or whatever is needed to treat a disease. Yamanaka factors show potential to reset not just cells, but the entire epigenome; they can send sirtuins back home and help restore the identity of malfunctioning cells.

In the future, drugs carrying the Yamanaka factors will be developed and used to switch on reprogramming genes. Taken by people in their mid-forties, these drugs will halt and reverse the signs of aging, including wrinkles, gray hair, vision loss, and mental decline. Patients on this regimen will feel progressively younger—people in their 40s will feel as if they are 25—and, consequently, discontinue treatment. They will start another cycle of treatment when signs of aging begin to reappear.

CHAPTER 7: THE AGE OF INNOVATION

Modern medicine works for most people, but not everyone. New technologies such as genome sequencing, data analytics, and artificial intelligence can be leveraged to get accurate test results and deliver precise treatment. These technologies are part of the mechanisms that will extend average healthy lifespan in coming years.

Key Takeaway: Genome sequencing is revolutionizing the future of medicine.

When the Human Genome Project was launched in 1990, it cost $10 to read one letter in the genome. It took 10 years and a few billion dollars to read the whole genome. Today, all 25,000 genes in the genome can be read in a few days for less than a hundred dollars.

DNA sequencing is revolutionizing medicine by giving researchers a better understanding of diseases, particularly cancer. Researchers can take cells from a tumor, read each of their DNA letters, analyze the chromatic structure and understand how old the tumor is, how it has grown, how it is mutating, and the bacteria that might protect it from anticancer drugs. Doctors may even be able to diagnose cancers with a simple blood test. They can scan blood for cell-free DNA and tell where an undetected cancer is growing in the body.

DNA sequencing can also tell us what foods to eat, what drugs our bodies will respond best to, and what therapies will maximize our potential lifespan. Genetic tests available today can tell which breast cancer patients will respond better to hormone treatments than to chemotherapy.

In the near future, drugs will be prescribed based on a patient's epigenetic age—people respond differently to treatment based on age, genetics, race, and other variations—and cancers will be treated based on their specific genetic mutation rather than their location in the body. We're edging closer to a time when doctors will not prescribe drugs until they know a patient's epigenome. People may not even have to wait until they are sick; genomes will be sequenced and ran against a database to find potential health risks as observed in people with similar gene types and combinations.

Key Takeaway: Biotrackers are key to optimizing health and boosting longevity.

We already have watches that measure heart rate and body temperature and track movement and sleep cycles. Many athletes wear biosensing tech that tracks how their bodies respond to diet, training, and stress. Today, researchers are working on sensors that can identify diseases and injuries through sweat. There are companies developing breath analyzers that can detect inflammatory diseases and even cancer.

Miniature wearables and under-skin implants coming out in the near future will track not just the vital signs, but the oxygen in your blood, your vitamin balance, and thousands of other biomarkers. Combined with tech that gathers bio data through everything from the movement of your body to the tone of voice, these wearables and implants will diagnose diseases before you even feel unwell. There will be devices that tell you what foods to eat and what to avoid, when and how much to exercise, and when to meditate or tweak your air conditioner. Easy-to-miss conditions will be easily noticed when your biomarkers are tracked all the time.

PART III: WHERE WE'RE GOING (THE FUTURE)

CHAPTER 8: THE SHAPE OF THINGS TO COME

When DNA monitoring and biotracking technologies come of age, they will add about a decade of healthy lifespan to the current life expectancy. People will come to see that aging is not inevitable and begin to take better care of their bodies. Eating well and being active will add five more years to the life expectancy, embracing procedures that activate longevity genes will add eight years, and taking compounds that reset the genome will add ten years. In total, we will have 33 years of additional healthspan. Add to the current life expectancy (80 in most developed countries), and you are looking at a not-too-distant future where the average person lives to be 113 years old.

These are, of course, conservative estimates. There is no telling what will happen when the thousands of research studies and technologies people are working on merge. At the current pace of research and medical evolution, even if only a few of these interventions pan out, half of all children born in the US today can expect to live to 104. In another century, the average age will be 150. After that, the epigenome could be reset an indefinite number of times.

Key Takeaway: The transition to longer lives will worsen environmental degradation.

Reports that have analyzed dozens of scientific projections conclude that the planet can only sustain 8 billion people. In 2010, the late physicist Stephen Hawking estimated that mankind has about 100 years to find another planet to live. The problem isn't so much a growing population as it is our consumption and waste. Americans today consume three times as much food as they need to survive and produce 4.4 pounds of trash per person per day, only a third of which decomposes or is recycled. As a consequence, global warming is worsening at an unprecedented pace. Species are being driven to extinction, food webs are being destroyed, and floods, hurricanes, and droughts are getting severe.

An extended lifespan will mean more crowding, more consumption, more waste, and, consequently, more environmental damage.

Key Takeaway: Longer lifespan will mean less social progress and less social security.

New truths are accepted because older people—usually the population segment that opposes change—die off and new generations that are more receptive to new ideas take their place. As people live longer and the population of senior citizens grows, the culture and ideas that steer social progress will evolve at a slower pace.

Additionally, social security and pension programs will be severely strained as people live longer. In the years following the Second World War, there were 41 workers paying into Social Security for every beneficiary, in part because there were few Americans over the age of 65. Today, about three-quarters of Americans who reach the age of 21 will live to be 65, a good number of whom will go on to add two more decades to their lives. The ratio of workers to beneficiaries has fallen to three to one, which is almost unsustainable. Worse, current recommendations to make Social Security sustainable have not considered the possibility of a significant number of people living to be 120.

The pressure of not being able to meet the needs of an aging population will spill over to and strain health care, education, and disability compensation. As it is, there are no economic plans in place to prepare for a world in which people live 40-plus years in retirement—nothing that accounts for their health care needs, savings, or how the labor market will have to change. There is no plan for what will happen when people spend half of their lives in retirement.

Key Takeaway: Mankind will renovate in response to a growing population and make the world an even better place.

There is a case to be made that the consequences of a longer lifespan are not be all gloom and doom, and history proves it. Since the 1860s, life expectancy in the United Kingdom has more than doubled owing largely to the public health, education, and infrastructure investments that have been made in response to the challenges of a growing population. Globally, the last 200 years has seen an unprecedented population explosion, and this growth has coincided with falling rates of poverty, more stable access to food and shelter, better education and medical care, and greater access to clean water and electricity. A growing, longer-lived population has been the catalyst to social, economic, and political progress.

Population models that estimate the earth's carrying capacity get it wrong because they do not factor in human ingenuity. Thomas Malthus, who predicted in 1798 that living standards would nosedive because human population growth would outpace agricultural production, was wrong precisely for this reason. If anything, extending lifespan, or delaying death, will have not a very significant impact on population. The ongoing fall in birth rates is likely to counter the population effect of people living longer. Even if we were to end all deaths today, we would only have an additional 55 million people in the world a year. Human population will continue to grow, but by slower margins every subsequent year.

Extending healthy lives will mean that people will stay longer in the workforce and increase returns on society's investment in education and infrastructure. A longer healthspan will also reduce pressure on public health systems. Outside paid work, older people could still give back to society through mentorship and volunteering.

CHAPTER 9: A PATH FORWARD

Research into the biology of aging gets less than 1 percent of the total US medical research budget because aging has not yet been defined as a disease. The National Institutes for Health and other research funding agencies are eager to fund novel therapies that may end heart disease, cancer, and Alzheimer's disease (diseases that impact about 12, 9, and 3 percent of the population, respectively) but not aging, which disables 93 percent of people over the age of 50. It would be cheaper and more effective to address the root cause of all diseases than to address one disease at a time.

Key Takeaway: Defining aging as a disease will speed up the innovations that will prolong healthy lifespan.

Defining aging as a disease will attract more private and public investment, which will speed up the pace at which the therapies that slow or halt aging are being made. Major research institutes will have labs dedicated to the science of aging. This will be a major turning point for aging research because, today, there are more scientists eager to work on aging than there are labs to accommodate them. The first country to declare aging a disease will attract scientists and drug makers, create jobs, and realize significant returns on investment from being an industry leader.

If age is defined as a disease, doctors will be comfortable prescribing novel longevity drugs to older patients. They will rely less on age as a determinant of the quality of medical care they give. They will not limit treatment options for older patients or send them away with their pain and frailty because it is "natural" for people their age. Older and younger patients will be treated with the same interventions and the same enthusiasm.

EDITORIAL REVIEW

David A. Sinclair's *Lifespan: Why We Age—and Why We Don't Have To* is a dense exposition of aging and longevity research, the interventions and technologies that will extend average and maximum healthspan in coming years, and the social, economic, and ethical challenges society will have to grapple with when people begin to live to a hundred years and beyond.

Many of the ideas Sinclair presents in this tome are not new. As far back as 1987, research-scientists Durk Pearson and Sandy Shaw were demonstrating—in their National bestseller *Life Extension: A Practical Scientific Approach*—the potential of calorie restriction to boost lifespan. Aubrey de Grey and Michael Rae, in their 2007 book *Ending Aging*, were some of the early voices that popularized the view that aging is a treatable disease and not an inevitable part of life. Like Sinclair, de Grey and Rae were emphatic that the government should increase funding for aging research to match funding for other major diseases. And journalist Bill Gifford's 2015 *Spring Chicken* covers the gamut of aging research, including the longevity pathways we can unlock to live longer.

What's new is the grand theory of aging Sinclair espouses and what it means for humanity. Aging, Sinclair argues, is not caused by DNA mutations, mitochondrial disfunction, stem-cell exhaustion, or any of the other hallmarks of aging. And it can't be effectively treated by addressing any or all of these hallmarks, as many scientists and medical professionals are inclined to try. Rather, aging is the result of the epigenetic noise that accumulates over years of cellular insult. It can be slowed, halted, or reversed by activating the gene circuit that counters this noise.

What places Sinclair's work ahead of the pack is the fact that he is not just another scientist or curious journalist; he is a world-famous geneticist with nearly three decades of aging research under his belt and one of *Time*'s most influential people. Some of the most promising leads in aging research have been discovered by people working in his lab at Harvard Medical School or by scientists he has a close working relationship with.

Sinclair documents dozens of yeast and animal studies that his lab and other leading facilities have made to manipulate the epigenome and boost health and vitality, slow down and reverse aging, and extend longevity. He mentions a few human studies that have demonstrated the potential of intermittent fasting, calorie restriction, and intense exercise to achieve similar results. To cap it all, he reveals the supplements he takes and the lifestyle choices he makes to stay healthy and live longer. His 80-year father, who is on regimen similar to his, has returned to work and is enjoying good health and living a life of adventure.

What's notably different about Sinclair's work is the optimism he exudes. At a time when popular biologists such as Josh Mitteldorf—co-author of *Cracking the Aging Code*—consider aging an evolutionary necessity we can't really do much about, Sinclair imagines an exciting new world where no one has to age. A world where we can reverse organ damage, get rid of the senescent cells that slow us down, and reprogram genes so that we are immune to the wrinkles, disease, and frailty we associate with age. Yet, his work is not another elusive search for the Holy Grail of immortality. His only interest is to find ways to help people live meaningful, healthy lives and die with dignity.

Lifespan makes for an excellent introduction to many topics in biochemistry, including how genetics and longevity-enhancing pharmaceuticals work. At times, the writing is dense and loaded with technical jargon, but most of the book is easily accessible by a lay audience. Sinclair could have done without the seemingly endless anecdotes and personal experiences he conveys—or the near-constant talk about how important aging research is and how it is unrecognized and underfunded—but some of this fluff is what paints for the reader a complete picture of where we are and where we are going.

BACKGROUND ON DAVID ANDREW SINCLAIR

David Andrew Sinclair is an Australian biologist, inventor, author, and professor of genetics at Harvard Medical School. He is also the cofounder of the journal *Aging*, cofounder of the Academy for Health and Lifespan Research, and codirector of the Paul F. Glenn Center for the Biological Mechanisms of Aging.

Born in 1969, Sinclair grew up in New South Wales in Sydney, Australia. He obtained a Bachelor of Science at the University of New South Wales and a Ph.D. in Molecular Genetics from the same school. He worked as a postdoctoral researcher at M.I.T before moving to Harvard Medical School to teach aging biology.

Sinclair has published nearly 200 scientific papers, co-filed more than 50 patents, and cofounded more than a dozen biotechnology companies. He also chairs the scientific boards of advisers of several biotech companies. His work has been featured in numerous media outlets, including the TV shows *60 minutes* and *Through the Wormhole*. He has received 35 honors, including the Australian Medical Research Medal, and was named in *Time* magazine's 2014 list of the most influential people in the world. In 2018, he was named an Officer of the Order of Australia for his research into the biology of aging and lifespan extension.

*** END OF BOOK SUMMARY ***

If you enjoyed this SNAP Summary, we encourage you to purchase a copy of <u>the original book.</u>

We'd also love an honest review on Amazon.com!

> Want FREE book summaries delivered weekly? Sign up for our email list and get notified of all our new releases, free promos, and $0.99 deals!
>
> **No spam, just books.**

Sign up at www.snapsummaries.com

Made in the USA
Monee, IL
13 February 2022